Introduce Your Studen[t] [to Creative] [W]riting
A Guide for Parents and Teachers

China Adventures! *Revisited Revised*

By
Marcy Wirth
and
Edna Siniff

Meadow Hills

About Story

"China Adventures!" is written by children using a creative writing process developed by Edna Siniff, pulblisher and Lead Second Grade Teacher, Marcy Wirth. The cover on the facing page is the original design of the book titled "China Adventures!" It is reproduced on the following pages as an example of what can be created by Childeren.

Both Edna and Marcy worked within the required teaching guidelines of the school district and received tremendous support from the parents.

The human mind is designed to want answers to questions. This project enhances that theory.

Future employers want good communicatiors. Students who delvelop writing and reading skills will meet those needs.

ISBN13: 978-1-937162-23-8

Meadow Hills
Marine on St. Croix
Minnesota

China Adventures!

Marcy Wirth's
Second Grade Class
Scandia
Elementary
School

Edna and Marcy

The weekly guidelines, beginning on page 46, are based on the creation of the story "China Adventures!" Marcy worked with the whole class developing the skills needed to write. Plus all the other umpteen things a teacher does each day. Marcy found Journal writing very important in the process of learning to read and write. Each child used a yellow legal pad as their journal for their research.

Edna had 15 minutes, once a week, with each group of 4 to 5 students. This is where student ideas were discussed and expanded. Where individual creativity was encouraged and writing reviewed. Where items from indigenous people in other parts of the world were introduced. The concept was to create a story based on lands beyond the United States. In the process the students would broaden their knowledge while discovering things that might peak their interest. The student's research discoveries surprised everyone.

At the end of each day that Edna visited the class, Marcy and Edna reviewed the class experiences and writing process. Then planned together the next steps each would cover.

A Word from the Teacher

My class has been learning how to write, for different reasons, with methods used in today's classrooms.

Edna Siniff graciously agreed to come every Wednesday to guide my class in writing an exciting adventure story. She read a children's adventure book to stimulate their imaginations. We aligned our teaching with the strong developmental stage of imaginations in children ages 6-9.

That book used a time portal in the story. My class decided to go to China using a time portal as transportation!

They now write and write and are enthusiastic about developing a book. What a joy to see them explore creative writing.

What a gift Edna has given my students!

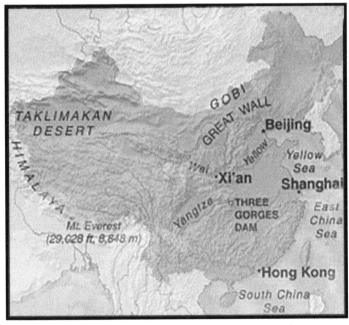

Map students found used to plan their trip to China.

Class Writing Project

Lindsey was fascinated with the history of the Titanic. She chose to write about Molly Brown who survived the sinking of that ship. With the help of her parents she learned about the museum at Molly Brown's House in Colorado. Lindsey came to class with printouts of the house. Her knowledge stimulated her classmate's interest in the museum. It seemed natural for them to use the wood-burning stove in Molly's kitchen as the portal for their adventure.

Sarah and her family traveled to China to visit their relatives several times. Sarah's culture and her visits to China created a natural curiosity for China in her classmates. Sarah's mother made Chinese dumplings for the class to eat, giving everyone a real taste of China.

Each student's personal interests became a guide for the subjects they researched for writing. Dinosaurs, the Rain Forest, Mt. Everest, Beijing and the Great Wall of China were the subjects of greatest interest.

In addition to the students having access to the library and the Internet for their research, they and their First Grade Buddies viewed "Wild China," a documentary produced by the BBC.

Every child in the class wrote a story about going to the Molly Brown Museum, passing through the portal, their character's events in China and return to the museum. Those stories were woven together by Edna, with assistance from the students. With the exception of transitions and editing for grammar and continuity, all the words are as the students wrote them.

Lindsey wrote the story on Molly Brown. Cari wrote most of the part involving Ray Chapman Anderson. Many of the children had similar places and/or events in their stories. Several were curious about the Yeti. Their facts and stories were combined to expand each chapter and provide story enhancement.

With the exception of Steven's story, all the student's characters traveled to China. Steven's interest in bowling took him to Egypt.

His contribution stands alone.

The thrill for the teachers came as Edna read the completed manuscript to the class. As each child recognized his or her own words, a broad smile crossed their faces and an arm motion or thumbs up signified their joy. Excitement filled the room.

Everyone knew, eighteen new writers were on their way to a life time of reading and writing.

The students met with Edna in small writing groups.

*The Molly Brown House Museum in Denver, Colorado.
Learning about Molly Brown and this museum
stimulated the class to begin their adventure here.*

Photo by Jody Wirth

Molly Brown

One day Molly Brown was baking a pie while her children, Helen and Larry, were playing outside. When they came in they asked, "Mom, can we have some pie?" And Molly Brown said,

"No, this is for your aunts and uncles."

"Yea," exclaimed the children.

"Do you think they will bring us presents?" Asked Larry.

"Don't always expect presents. When I was little..." The opening of the door interrupted Molly.

"Hello everyone! Good to see you!" Shouted the aunts and uncles.

"Did you bring us something?" asked Helen.

"Of course! We always bring you something," answered the uncles.

"What is it?" isked Larry happily. He was very happy.

"Wait! Let's go to dinner first!" interrupted Molly Brown.

When they got to the table, the kids received their presents and at dinner.

That evening the company and family sat by the fire and told some stories.

As the years passed and the kids grew up and left home J.J. Brown, Molly's husband, was not happy anymore. He finally decided to move back to Leadville, and away from Molly. With J.J. gone the house felt very empty to Molly. She decided to travel to Europe.

While in Europe she learned that her grandson was very sick. She decided it was time to come back to the United States. She boarded the Titanic in England. It was the first voyage of that ship. During the night the Titanic hit an iceberg and Molly nearly passed away. Luckily, she was able to get into a life boat and was rescued. She went back to live in her home in Denver.

Molly Brown House Museum

Molly Brown's house is a museum today.
That is where this 2nd grade class adventure begins.

The museum with parking lot.

Chapter One

Visitors to the Molly Brown Museum in Denver, Colorado

One warm summer morning many people were lining up to enter the Molly Brown Museum. Most of the visitors drove to the museum. One big group of school kids arrived by bus. They were on a field trip. Sam, Steven and Abby arrived at Molly Brown's museum with the kid's on a field trip.

Some, like Annie walked to the place where Molly Brown once lived. When they got there they saw Molly Brown, or someone who looked like her.

Annie said, "I see Molly Brown!"

"Really?" said Abby. The person they saw was a tour guide dressed like Molly Brown.

Amy and her sister Brooke, who is turning 16, flew in an airplane from Florida to Colorado for Brooke's birthday. When they got to Denver, they headed for the Molly Brown Museum.

They were excited when they walked into the museum and saw a picture of Molly Brown.

"She is very beautiful," said Amy.

"She is," answered Brooke.

Maggie Olson is an eight-year-old girl visiting the Museum with her mother." As Maggie and her mother got out of the car her mother asked, "Well ... did you know that this is where Molly Brown lived?

Maggie couldn't wait to go inside the Museum. She ran up the steps, one foot after the other.

Just as Amy and Brooke walked up the steps to

join a very long line waiting to go in, Maggie Olson ran passed them.

Amy

"Look," said Amy. Up ahead of them they saw Molly Brown! Well, they thought they saw her but it was just another woman.

In the museum they saw a very interesting painting of Molly Brown. Amy thought it was great but went to another room. She smelled something very good. She thought it smelled like a cherry pie coming right out of the oven. Amy followed her nose to the kitchen.

Maggie's mom said, "Let's go to the kitchen." "Yah!" shouted Maggie. She ran faster than she ever had!

"Hey," Mom shouted, " Slow down!"

The people visiting the museum were put into groups. Alexie and Maggie were with the guide, Molly Brown. As Amy entered the kitchen, she joined them.

Lily and her cousin Britney were going to Florida. But they got on the wrong plane, it was going to Colorado and the pilot said they were about to land in Denver. Since they had to wait 24 hours for a plane to take them to Florida they decided to rent a car and do some sightseeing.

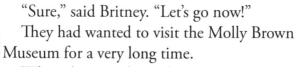
Maggie

Alexie

Lily asked Britney, "Can we go to the museum of Molly Brown's house?"

Lily

"Sure," said Britney. "Let's go now!"

They had wanted to visit the Molly Brown Museum for a very long time.

When they got there, they went in the house and found their way into the kitchen just as the guide started talking.

There are a lot of people in this room, thought, Lily.

A child named Alexie lived in Pennsylvania. She was going on a vacation with her mother. Alexie was so excited! As soon as they were both packed, they got in the car and were off!

When they got to Molly Brown's Museum, there was a nice man at the door. He asked Alexie how old she was. She said she was eight years old. When Alexie went into the museum she was so amazed.

"Wow!" she said.

"Yes," her mom said. "It is very amazing."

Right in front of them was a model of Molly Brown. Alexie slipped away from her mother and through a doorway. Then she figured out that she was in a kitchen. She saw an oven with a cherry pie in it. The baking pie made the room smell wonderful. Alexie saw other kids walk into the room. They were looking at the picture of Molly Brown. So she joined them. A girl named Amy mentioned they could look in the oven.

Eight year-old Jack had no brothers or sisters. He and his parents were on their vacation in Colorado. Uncle Todd was on a very long trip when he met his brother and nephew at Molly Brown's house.

Jack was looking at Molly Brown's lifeline. A girl standing next to him also found this history interesting. The guide asked them to move into the kitchen. Jack and the girl, who was Annie, joined the group led by the Molly Brown guide.

Jack was surprised to find Sam standing by the stove in the kitchen. They were best friends since preschool! They liked looking at all the old things that told the story of the sinking of the Titanic.

Jason lives in British Columbia in Canada. He was doing a report on the Titanic. So his dad brought him to Molly Brown's house in Denver, Colorado. As soon as they were inside, Jason's Dad took him to the kitchen.

13

Chapter Two

The Kitchen

The smell of something very good was coming from the kitchen. It smelled like a cherry pie coming right out of the oven

The tour guide, who looked like Molly Brown, was standing near the old stove when the museum visitors entered the kitchen. She described the old kitchen and the old wood-burning kitchen stove.

"Wow," said Abby, "look at that stove."

A group of kids stood around the old stove. Lily went to see what was in the oven. The tour guide opened the oven door and pulled out a cherry pie! "Come over here to the table and sit," she called to her tour group as she carried the pie to the kitchen table. Most of the adults in the room followed the guide.

But Maggie, Abby and Lily stayed by the old-fashioned stove with Amy and Alexie. Another group of kids saw the oven at the same time. Jason, Sam, Jack, and Annie came to look inside. They were standing very close to the old stove.

"I love old antiques!" said Maggie.

"Me too!" said Lily.

Jason said, "I wonder how the oven works?"

They all peeked into the oven .

Lilly

Jack

Alexie

Alayna

Abby

Jason

Amy

Maggie

Steven

Annie

Sam

and suddenly...

VANISHED!

Maggie and Baibai on the Great Wall of China.

Chapter Three

China

In a blink of the eye Maggie was floating in a tunnel of purple smoke. When the smoke cleared she found herself on a silky patch of grass near a big city.

"Hey!" She said. " Where am I? …Mom!" She screamed with fear!

"You are in China," said a small voice.

Maggie launched to her feet. Facing her was a young girl with dark black hair.

"Who are you?" Maggie asked.

"My name is Baibai," she said.

"Where do you live?"

"I live in Beijing," Baibai said.

"Do you want to come to the Parade?" The young Chinese girl asked.

"Yes," answered Maggie. The two girls started off down a path.

"Are you sure you know the way?" Maggie asked.

"Yes... Of course I know the way," she said.

Amy landed on the Great Wall of China. Amy looked around and saw lots of children around her. All of the kids were impressed. "Where am I?" she asked. One of the children, a Chinese girl answered, "We are on the Great Wall of China."

"The Great Wall of China?" shouted Amy. She was surprised. "WOW, I have never seen the Great Wall of China."

All of the brave Chinese children gathered around the newcomer.

The tallest dark haired girl said, "My name is Singsing." As Sinsing introduced her companions. Amy told them her name too.

17

Singsing continued, "This is Chris, his Chinese name is Bat but he doesn't like it, so I don't mention it."

"This is Liesa. Her Chinese name is Beibei."

"Here is Grant. His Chinese name is Suiesuie."

"This is Aleina. Her Chinese name is Meimei."

Amy walked with her new Chinese friends to their homes and went inside Singsing's home. Singsing dressed Amy in Chinese clothes that looked like blue cover-ups.

"Your house is so beautiful," said Amy. There were a lot of plants. The children ate a lot of Chinese food. The dumplings tasted so good.

"Amy saw two dogs that were very big in the car by the house.

They are my Uncle's dogs, Crabby and Dane," said Singsing. They were the same age and liked to play with a tennis ball. Abby let them out of the car and Crabby ran away. Then Dane lay down and rested. Dane is the lazy one of the two dogs. Amy chased Crabby to make him come back. He ran so fast Amy had to collapse to the ground. Then a Chinese man came over and started to speak weird. Amy could not understand him. She got up and ran to a woman who

could translate for her. The translator said that the Chinese guy asked, "Are you all right?"

"Tell him, yes, thank you." said Amy.

Crabby finally came back and Amy and her Chinese family went to a Festival. While they were walking down a narrow street Amy saw a red dragon coming toward them. Near the dragon was a girl like herself.

When Maggie and her friend, Baibai, got to the city they saw the coolest thing... It was a red dragon. There were so many lights. There were fireworks.

Then the dragon blew fire from his mouth and frightened them.

Maggie ran from the dragon and bumped into Amy.

Amy and Maggie found each other.
Maggie said, "I want to go home."

Baibai lit a firecracker.
Yellow smoke swirled around Maggie and Amy.
When the smoke cleared the two girls were gone.

Chapter Four

Dinosaur Egg

Abby was in China! She looked around. She had landed on the Great Wall of China! No one was near her. She wanted to get to a village, but which way should she go? She was lost and alone on the Great Wall of China.

"Oh, no," she said out loud, "I need help! …

Abby walked and walked then she saw a village! Near the village she saw a sign.

She had no idea what it said. At that moment a book appeared! It was on the ground by the signpost. Large letters on the cover read "China," in English! She opened the book and looked for the Chinese word that matched the sign. She found it.

The sign meant Rainforest.

"I want to see that," she said. Abby followed the path into the forest. The trees were filled with animals and the rivers had amazing animals too! It was cool!

She walked and walked. She looked around and around. Now there were people everywhere! Abby wanted to know more about the Rainforest. So she opened the book and looked up Rainforest. Just as she was about to read, a herd of camels came by. She secretly followed them. They stopped at a dirt land. Abby started exploring.

Then someone saw her. "Get over here!" shouted the man.

Abby ran away from him. The man ran after her. Abby ran as fast as she could! She could hear him getting closer. She looked back and couldn't see him. So, she hid behind a rock. The man ran right passed her and was gone. When she thought it was safe Abby got out and ran the other way.

The path she followed took her to an archaeological dig. As she explored the dig she bumped into someone! "Oh no," she said. She looked up. It was Ray Chapman Anderson!

She talked to him. "You're the Dinosaur man, aren't you?"

"That I am," he said.

Then Abby helped him look for dinosaur bones. She was watching when he found an egg! He kept the egg and they left the dig. He said that he would show her the way back to the time machine! They walked and walked.

"I forgot how to get there," said Ray. They were lost.

"It's at the Great Wall of China," said Abby.

They rested for a minute. Then moved on. They saw all kinds of stuff too. They walked and walked many miles. Then Abby asked,

"How many miles did we walk?"

"We walked 1,252 miles!" said Ray.

Abby looked at the sky. The sun was setting. They walked some more. It got hot. She was sweating.

It was almost the end of the day when they came to a pond. Ray got a bucket and filled it with water and poured it out on himself. Abby did the same. The water felt good. Abby and Ray walked four more miles.

As they reached the Great Wall of China a bright light flashed and Ray Chapman Anderson was alone.

Chapter Five

Jack and Sam Look for Mt. Everest

Jack and Sam landed on a different part of the Great Wall of China. No other people were near them. The boys looked around. They saw an open market. Jack was hungry. Sam was too. So, they bought food and gobbled down the tasty Chinese Dumplings.

That night they went to sleep in the hut that was higher up on the wall. When they got up they went back to the market to eat breakfast, it was awesome.

"OK, think of an ancient place in China!" said Jack. "How about Mount Everest," said Sam. "Why don't we go there?" He asked.

"Good Idea," said Jack. "But that will take months," protested Sam.

"We could rent bikes," said Jack.

"Perfect," said Sam.

So Jack and Sam rented some bikes.

Jack and Sam rode and rode.
On the way they found a book about Mount Everest!
"Hey look it's a book," said Sam. So he started to read.
"There is a monster called the Yeti," explained Sam.
"We should be careful," said Jack.
They finally reached Mount Everest and began to climb. As they
climbed around a sharp rock Sam lost his footing and began to
slide. Jack tried to catch him but began sliding too.

They slide down the mountain to a cave.

"Hey look, candles," said Sam.
"I found a match!" Said Jack.
"Where should we go?" questioned Sam.
"How about in this cave," said Jack.

So they lit the candles and went into the cave.

"What's that?" Asked Sam.
"I believe that is the Yeti."
"THE YETI?!?!?"

"It's OK Sam, it is just a baby monkey!" said Jack.
The monkey ran deeper into the cave. Jack and Sam followed it.

Lights and movement ahead of them made Jack and Sam hide behind a wall in the cave. It looked like a torch was burning. The shadows on the ceiling of the cave looked like a huge gorilla was waving its arms.

It sounded like the animal was having fun.

The boys moved slowly toward the shadows.

Yeti !!!!

Chapter Six

It Looks Like China

Annie · Alexie

Annie and Alexie looked inside the stove, and shut their eyes. When they opened them they were in China, on the Great Wall.

Annie asked, "How could this be?"

Alexie said, "The stove must be a time portal."

"Wow!" Said Annie.

"It looks like China," said Alexie.

"China is the only place you can find the Great Wall of China. Did you know that Beijing is the capital of China?" asked Annie.

"There sure are lots of people in China," answered Alexie. "They are walking so fast."

"I wonder why," said Annie.

They finally figured out why. It was because everyone loved the Great Wall of China.

Annie wanted to see all around China.

"Look at this huge water fall," said Alexie,

"I wish we could slide on it," said Annie.

"Oh my," said Alexie, "look at the ducks and the horses."

"Hey, come and look at this. It looks like a note. It says:

Come to Mount Everest.
From the Yeti.

On the back it said....

Come to china right now.
From Alayna

"I know what we should do," said Alexie. "You go to Beijing and I'll go see the Yeti. Here's a cell phone, call me when you are done."

"OK," said Annie. "Bye, bye."

They split up.

Alexie walked all the way to Mount Everest and started climbing. She followed a trail up the slope trying to catch up to the team of climbers ahead of her.

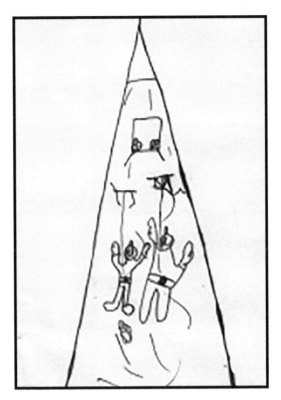

Suddenly her feet slipped and she slid

down the mountain into a cave.

Meanwhile, Annie noticed there was a dirt road under her feet as she walked to the city. "Wow!" she said, "I'm in Beijing! I think I'll explore." So she started to explore the city. While she was walking she said to herself, "while I'm exploring I'll look for my friends." Then Annie saw a library, "I'm going to check out some books," she said aloud. Just before she stepped into the library she saw an old woman.

"Hello," said the old voice. "I am Alayna."
"Hi," said Annie.
Alayna said, "Come with me to the market."

There were people everywhere in the market. One person in the market was selling books.

Lilly

"Look. That's a big book!! said Lilly.
"Open it." She was talking to the owner when Annie walked up to her.
"Hi, I am Annie," she said. Lilly was surprised to see her.
"It's really been a bad day. We got on the wrong plane and landed in Colorado instead of Miami. Then I was looking at the stove in Molly Brown's House Museum and the next thing I knew, ...I was in China," said Lilly.
"I was in the museum too," said Annie.
Lilly looked down at the open book in her hands. "Look, is that a diamond," she asked.
"It's lighting up like a diamond," said Annie. Lilly picked up the shinning stone and held it in her hand.

"Alayna has been showing me the market. Why don't you come with me?" said Annie.
Lilly said, "No, I am going back to the Great Wall of China."
She said good-bye to Annie and walked away.

At the end of the day Annie found a Chinese charcoal stove. As Annie stared at the red coals in the stove

she disappeared!!

Chapter Seven

Meeting Hillary and Norgay

Jason

Jason was watching the guide pull the pie out of the oven. He looked behind him for his dad, but his dad was not there. He looked in the oven again.

Jason blinked and was at the bottom of Mt. Everest!

Mt. Everest is five and a half miles above sea level and is located on the border of Nepal and Tibet. In Nepal the people call Mt. Everest Sagarmatha which means "Goddess of the Sky." People in Tibet call Mt. Everest Chomolungma which means "Mother Goddess of the Universe."

Jason saw some Sherpas and asked them to take him to the top. They said, "OK." The Sherpas were climbing with Sir Edmund Hillary and Tensing Norgay who were the first to climb Mt. Everest.

Jason started climbing up the mountain. It started to get hard to breathe! Finally the team was at the top!!!

As soon as they were at the top, a strong gust of wind blew Jason down the side of the peak and into a cave!

He heard a weird noise. It went, "aaaahhhh"! The noise got louder and louder. Finally he saw what was making the noise! It was the Yeti! Jason was very, very, very scared! But then he saw a light. He ran to it. It was a torch.

Jason found Alexie pressed against the wall of the cave watching the Yeti dance.

"Hi," said the Yeti. "You're just in time for the party!"

"Oh!" Said Jason. "Then let's party." And they all started to dance.

Suddenly a monkey jumped up on the Yeti. The Yeti and the monkey danced more.

Jack and Sam came into the light and saw Alexie and Jason dancing with the Yeti.

"It looks like a party," said Jack.
"Hi," said Alexie. "The Yeti is so friendly."
Jason asked, "Where did you come from?"
"From Molly Brown's House Museum," said Sam as he started to dance with them.

The monkey jumped off the Yeti and grabbed a box that was on the floor. Jack, Sam, Alexie and Jason looked at the monkey as he opened the box. Instantly the Yeti and monkey were alone in the cave.

Chapter Eight

Steven and the Egyptian Game of Bowling

All of a sudden "poof," Steven disappeared from the kitchen. He found himself in a very strange place. He was in ancient Egypt where bowling was invented.

Steven

Steven loves to bowl, so he picked up a bowling ball and rolled it toward the pins. All the pins fell down. The people around him shouted,
   "Steven! You got a strike."

He was so excited that he jumped in the air and when he came down he was in the kitchen of Molly Brown's house.

Chapter Nine

Adventurers Return

As Abby's eyes cleared from the bright flash she found she was back in the Museum with all the other kids and her mom. "Wow," she said. "I met the greatest dinosaur man."

Jack, Sam, Alexie and Jason vanished back to the old oven.
"It must have been a magical monkey!" said Jack as they stood by the old stove.
"Maybe it was the box that was magical," said Alexie.
"That was amazing," exclaimed Jack.
"That was a wonderful trip," said Sam.

The last memory Annie had of China was looking at the red coals in the old charcoal stove.
"Come on Annie," said her Mom. Annie was staring at the red glow coming from Molly Brown's oven. Her mother's voice made her look around.
"Mom, this is an amazing place," said Annie.

Lilly went back to the Great Wall of China. On the way she bought a balloon from a nearby store to make herself feel better. When she reached the Great Wall she climbed as high as she could. Lilly's balloon actually made her float out of China and back into Molly Brown's house. As she stood in front of the old stove she remembered the small shining stone she found in the big book.
"Was it real," she asked. She opened her hand and there it was.

In a split second the yellow smoke from Baibai's firecracker carried Maggie and Amy to Molly Brown's kitchen where Maggie's mom was eating cherry pie.

"Really Maggie come on," her mom said. Maggie smiled and said, "This is a magical day!"

Everyone was right where each had been.
Conversation continued as if the children had
never left the room.

The End!

Things We Learned About China

As the project came to an end the students wanted to list some of the things they learned about China while researching for their writing. Here are their "facts."

It is a huge place and has strange landscapes.

Beijing is the capitol.

The 2008 Summer Olympics were held in Beijing.

The China road is an old trade route.

There are colorful places with big flowers and harsh places.

Some places get to 40° below zero and are ice bound half the year.

Ice fishing happens on the Black Dragon River.

There are huge waterfalls and beautiful flowers.

There are places where it rains lots. Likr four months of daily rain.

There are Wild Birds: Cranes and ducks on Swan Lake.

The Crane is called the bird of God.

The people catch fish in nets. Many places are over fished.

Gobi Desert is in China.

There are Bamboo forests.

The Great Wall of China was built to protect the people from invasion.

They were invaded a lot.

Over one million people died building the Great Wall of China.

People go over rivers on chairs in the mountains.

Nomads have tents to move with their herds.

They do group living.

People ride bikes.

Women are caretakers.

Women take care of reindeer.

There are horse herds and horse races, big herds of sheep, and camels.

Pigs and wild boars eat walnuts.

Animals hibernate.

Some bats are smaller than a teacup.

China is home to Giant Pandas.

Red fox and the world's largest squirrel live in China.

Siberian Tigers live in China.

Tiger bones are made into medcine.

Some places have Elephants.

Mt. Everest was formed about 60 million years ago.

It is the tallest mountain in the world.

It is 5.5 miles above sea level, 29,035 feet.

It was named after Sir George Everest.

It is located on the border between Nepal and Tibet.

660 people have successfully climbed Mt. Everest.

In Nepal the mountain is called Sagarmatha. It means Goddess of the Sky.

People in Tibet call the mountain Chomolungma, the Mother Goddess of the Universe.

Sir Edmund Hillary and Tenzing Norgay were the first people to climb Mt. Everest.

All Eighteen Children in Marcy Wirth's Second Grade Class Participated

Jack	Alexis
Dominic	Abigail
Lindsey	Sarah
Talyr	Parker
Steven	Samuel
Nicholas	Erin
Alexis	Cari
Chloe	Adam
Samantha	Ashley

Study Guide Questions For China Adventures

Expanding their learning Experiences

1. Why do you believe there was a connection to the Titanic history as the story opened.
2. How do you think the children poofed into China?
   2.a. You know this was an imaginary adventure.
      Do you have different ways for them to time travel?
3. Did time stop for the other people in the museum?
4. What sort of feelings did the children experience in China?
5. How was it possible for the different children to find help in China?
6. Would you want to time travel?
   Where?
   Why?

Predictions:

1. Do you think the children would want to travel again?
   If so, where.
2. Which group of kids would you have liked to travel with?
   Why?
3. How would you get each group back to Molly Brown's House Museum from China?
4. When you saw the shadows in the cave, what did you see?

Projects:

1. Make a diorama of where one group landed.
2. Create a poster of the animals and people they met in China.
3. Make a game board showing the locations where each group traveled.
4. Create a cave out of cardboard then construct the images you saw in the shadows.

Enrichment:

Like the children who wrote China Adventures you can add to their findings with your research.

Marcy teaching students journal writing.

Journal Writing

Reading and writing, when taught together, increase a person's awareness of themselves and the world around them. During Journal Writing the students were able to connect their ideas to their writitng. Writing equals communication. You are preparing your students for the future.

Every year my students write and illustrate in their journals. This is a year long activity. Drawing helps stimulate and develop a vision for the ideas or subjects each student writes about.

The students turned small group working time into pure excitement and joy. By the power of their imaginations they developed the love of reading. Imginagtion allows the child to enter into the future.

The following journal entries were selected after the completion of "China Adventures." These examples were written near the end of the school year.

The journal entries were **not** edited or corrected. They show the quality of writing skills achieved by members of this class.

from, P

Our Class Book

A publisher came to teach how to write a book! We got this book called "Chocolate a Library Adventure!" The book that we are writing is about adventures in CHINA! First, we came up with ideas for the story, like Mount Everest, Beijing and even the Great Wall of China. Then we thought of the Characters could be teleparted when they were on summer vacation at Molly Brown's Museum when they looked into an old oven. Next, we thought of the characters. Then we each wrote our own story and she is weavinn them together! She said we had too many characters so we voted. We made pictures too. We made a great book!

From, S

Date

Our Class Book

When Edna, a publisher came
to our class she gave us a
book called Chocolate! A library
Adventure. After that, We were
going to make a book! I was
very excited. We sat down at

a table and shared our ideas.
We finally thought of what our
setting would be: in China and
Mount Everest. Edna also let
us watch a movie called: China.
We took notes about it. Edna
was one of the three to go to

New York. I think Edna
is a great and wonderful person.
She is so nice to all of us.
And she taught in Scandia in
this very same room! I am very
happy she could come here and
help us make our very own book!!

Class Writing Activity Plan
Beginning Activities

Preparation for writing project includes: basic writing skills for sentence structure.

Introduce the concept of creating a book.

Introduce legal note pads for recording research information and journal writing through out the year.

Week One

Begin reading a children's adventure story book that includes creative ways to travel long distances and introduce students to other cultures.

Talk about favorite things the students do at home.
List one activity you like doing. Student's favorite activity.
Write a sentence about that activity.
Chose a person with whom to do that activity.
Write a sentence with that person. (Team writing)

Week Two

Introduce dialogue for writing in student journals.
Use quote marks to identify when a person speaks. Two fingers on each side of their heads were wiggled when the child spoke. Made learning this skill fun.

Introduce objects from other places in the world.
Thses items may come from community members.
It is important to have items the children can handle.
Check with area museums to determine availability of items.
Edna's collection came from indigenous people of: Afghanistan, Africa, Alaska, Australia, Ireland, and New Zealand.
The students were allowed to handle the items and ask questions.
Purpose: To stimulate interest in other cultures.

Assignment:
List 3 ideas for a story and
List 3 character's names to be used in the story.
The ideas can be their own or can be ones mentioned by others.

Week Three

Have students list story ideas.

Discuss their ideas and ways to use them in their writing.

Discuss the character names from the student list.

Show more items from other places in the world if possible.

Find one story idea that all can write about in one paragraph.

Limit number of names for characters.

Week Four

Teach how to take notes on memo pads.

Vote on character's names from suggested list. Vote for three.

Read what students wrote.

Review the need to write in complete sentences and give characters a voice. Quote marks.

Keep items from other countries available for children to handle. This gives them opportunity to discover additional information or ask questions. These items are a reminder to research other cultures.

Assignment:

Continue writing their adventure, include dialogue

Week Five

Geography lessons on continents and United States

Vote on character names from revised list, based on last weeks vote.

Read the student's stories.

Discuss their ideas.

Introduce portal concept for the class writing project.

Create list for portal possibilities.

Assignment:

Think about the country the class will visit in their book's adventures.

Week Six

Computer visit to a choice country.

Each child shares the info learned during computer search.

Hand out character names.

Discuss the possible country ideas and adventures.

Learn where the interest is for each student.

Assignment:
Write one adventure using 2 characters on the list.

Week Seven

Each child reads adventure from last week's assignment.
Edit adventure and spell check.
Vote on the country to visit.
Computer visit to chosen country.(Volunteer types facts for all.)
Discuss country the class will explore.
Add to portal list.

Assignment:
Write adventure in the country the class chose.
Schedule a field trip to a museum.

Week Eight

6th Grade Buddies type adventure stories – use spell check.
Review interests of individuals.
Each child reads facts learned about China.
Discuss possible adventures in China.
Discuss locations the class story will begin.
Create list of possible portals.

Assignment:
Write adventure in China using characters selected by class.

Week Nine

Choose location for story to begin.
Give list of possible portals.
Listen to last weeks writing assignment.

Assignment:
Write complete story using location chosen by class. Have characters on adventure in China. Have characters find a portal to bring them back to the place the story begins.

Week Ten

Eat Chinese meal prepared by parents.
Choose beginning portal as a class.
Each child reads their story.
Critique of stories.

Assignment:
Check spelling and grammar.
Make sure there is conversation and description in each story.

Week Eleven

Discuss beginning portal.
Decide how to use portal at beginning.
Discuss facts in written stories, correct facts.
Students read their stories.
Critique of stories.

Week Twelve

Review each story with its author.

Assignment:
Write pieces needed to complete class story.
Create illustrations for stories.
Enter each story in the computer for transfer to adult's computer.

Week Thirteen

Read combined story to the class.
Collect their art and any additional writing.

Assembling the Story

Having knowledge of word processing software will make this task easier for the person assembling the story.

1. A few parents were able to type their Child's work, checked the spelling and emailed it to the volunteer assembling the class story. All student's stories were typed in Microsoft Word. Many were typed by sixth grade buddies.

2. Read all the student's stories. Identify the parts that fit the beginning, middle and end of the story.

3. In word processing software high light and copy the words in each story that fit the beginning of the class story. Place them in a new document with a name that represents the student's book story.

4. Make sure you mark the words chosen in each student document with color as you select them for a place in the book. Yellow works well. When the volunteer returns to that student's document, they will know which words have been used.

5. After all the beginning parts are placed in the combined document go through the students words looking for pieces that fit well together. Move the paragraphs and sentences in the document until the story line flows easily.

6. When the beginning of the class story reads easily move to the next section repeating the same process.

Many students will write about the same things. They get their ideas from each other and from the films and the books they used for research. Similar things go easily together. Character names are used to give continuity.

Use chapters to separate the different ideas the students write about.

When assembling the class story think of each student's writing as parts of a jigsaw puzzle. As the pieces flow together a complete story emerges.

The student illustrations are added in the final phase.

Weeks Fourteen and Fifteen

Scan the student art into a computer file. If printing at a commercial company the art should be scanned at 300 DPI and be smaller than the page of the book. i.e. If the printed page is 5.5 inches wide the art should be no more than 4 inches wide. You can set the scanner to the dimensions needed and also the DPI.

Students participate with a volunteer to choose and place scanned art in the story on the computer.

Adults help students proofread final draft of book.

Printing can be done on a copy machine.
If you use 8.5 by 11 inch paper you can print 2 pages on each side. Each page will be 5.5 inches wide and 8.5 inches high. The margins should be at least half an inch wide to allow space for binding the finished pages together.

*Edna and Marcy talking with the authors
at their signing party.*

Authors of "China Adventures!" hearing their combined stories for the first time.

Edna with students helping choose which story to insert.

Future employers want good communicators. Students who develop writing and reading skills will meet those needs.